Othername
Volum

Food Memory Marriage Alienation & Loss

Jetko
Morland-Chapman
Buckingham
Shaknes
Sheridan

0 9521806 3 4

Food Memory Marriage Alienation & Loss
Poems by Carla Jetko, Marise Morland-Chapman, Helen Buckingham, Natasha Shaknes and Laura Sheridan.

ISBN 0 9521806 3 4

Copyright (c) the authors 2004

British Library Cataloguing in Publication Data.
A catalogue record for this book is available from The British Library.

Published by Othername Press
14 Rosebank
Rawtenstall
Rossendale
BB4 7RD
email:othernamepress@yahoo.co.uk

The publishers and authors assert their usual rights with regard to reproduction and moral and ethical ownership of this material in line with current standards.

Printed by Kershaw Print
928 Burnley Road
Rossendale

Cover design and layouts by Kickstartists
Back cover photo by Marise Morland-Chapman

Editor's Note

In producing this volume the Editor is attempting to bring his karmic account back into credit after heavy withdrawals caused by resentment at receiving unsolicited manuscripts.

This book is dedicated to unsolicited poets, their hidden talents and unheard voices, with the gentle reminder that, like the writers collected here, it is usual to pursue magazine publication before stampeding towards a solo collection.

JCH May 2004

Hidden

Among the waves so big and the sea so small
A little voice shouts out
Crying for an unknown reason
Calling through the mist and sand
An answer comes from a hidden cove
And a dream is whisked from far away
Places and paradises
They call to each other and the dream is set
Where no one can find them

R. Hartley

Cover: version *I am Half-Sick of Shadows-said the Lady of Shalott* by J W Waterhouse; the original is in the Art Gallery of Ontario, Toronto Canada. See also jwwaterhouse.com

Contents	Page
Carla Jetko	5
Cruise Ship Delilah	6
The Kitchen Audabe	8
I am	9
The Button Box	10
Reasons	11
Marise Morland-Chapman	13
Screen Test	14
Encounter at Park Street	15
The Poet to his Muse	16
Reunion	17
Helen Buckingham	18
Future Past	19
It was Ruth Rendell's Birthday	20
Green Light	21
Four poems	22
Ocean View	23
Natasha Shaknes	24
An experience that was replaced	25
On a shaded foil	26
A circular disorder	27
A long apology	28
Communication of saviours	29
A dynamic temper	30
Laura Sheridan	31
Eternal Opera	32
David's Rooftop	33
Notes On The Forest	34
The Rejuvenation Of Grandma	37

Carla Jetko

is a Canadian poet living on the wild moors on the Isle of Mull, Inner Hebrides. She revels in performing her poetry and is also a gourmet chef, with food figuring prominently in many works. A hedonist, she has a penchant for velvet, emeralds, Bach's *Toccata and Fugue* and five-course meals. She has recently completed her first collection of poetry *The Body Banquet*, which is ready for publication. www.jetko.com

Cruise Ship Delilah

Aisle One; party favours, ice cream, frozen peas

This supermarket is her culinary cruise ship,
a metal-wheeled voyage from the orange sands
of butternut squash to the tea fields of Sri Lanka
where women's hands are stained from the picking.
Her purple painted fingernails push out
like tiny headstones from their lair of lace cuff
to snap a spine of celery in two.

Aisle Two; wines, spirits, turkey basters, shrunken heads

Delilah strolls the linoleum of her imaginary lido deck
fingering one olive in a dry martini,
sunning herself before the pictures of Portugal's Costa Verde
and the Italian villas' painted bright on bottles
of Chianti and Mateus.

Jetko

Aisle Three; gourmet counter, ethnic foods

She waits by the Cumberland sausages
for Mr. Elfinrod of the speciality cheese department.
He comes each trip,
to feed petit camembert, mini gorgonzola and baby edam
into the patient venus fly trap of her mouth.
She chews, as her cleavage struggles out of its nest
of Victorian satin and ribbons,
like some hungry Easter hat,
like a pair of feral peonies,
a floral decoupage on acid.

Aisle Four; paper products, perishables, melons, computers

He helps her with the shopping list, with quick, fawning gestures
his white hat bobbing beyond the prow of the cart
like a life raft,
as she prods a side of oak-smoked salmon,
gouges the eye out of an Egyptian potato,
as she trills to herself like the shrike,
the butcher bird,
after impaling its victim on the spikes of the blackthorn tree.

Jetko

Kitchen Aubade

When I woke up under the great plank table
I knew I would have to say goodbye;
kiss your purple painted eyelids
to the smell of bacon frying.

One cook was already scraping a cast iron pan
across a burner. His crepe-soled shoes
stepped on the spread of your black hair
but didn't wake you.
Your chest created gentle waves
under the garland of plastic gardenias.
I stole an apron off the Aga handle
and covered you.
I waited until everyone had left the room
and then crept out with a croissant crumbling warm in my mouth.

Jetko

I am

I am a handful of soft, red fruit. I sit heavy, waiting for you. Oozing sweetness, I sweat a love sweat. Red satined and chambered, I wait for the touch of the match, laying my tongue on the carpet like a fuse. I am a soft, red fruit exploding in your mouth. The taste of a Picasso painting all bulls and warm blood. I have a roundness that your hands need. Yielding spheres of feasty flesh. When I am touched, I hold back, willing you to devour me, like Eskimos lapping up the still-beating heart of a seal kill. Whole. Naked. I am heavy with want. I am ready.

Jetko

The Button Box

With a china doll and a hack saw, I entered the empty room. I would have to do this by myself. A careful pencil mark. A measurement, quick, with the tape my mother used for sewing and a special box to catch the head. This box once held a zillion buttons that were bought in bulk from a catalogue. A picture of a shy women in a field of flowers on the front. Porcelain splinters like rat's teeth embedded themselves in the material of my black suit jacket. The lady smiled when the head crashed into her world, all but crushing the lupins that grew under one tree. She straightened her bonnet and cradled the singing skull under one arm as she started up the hill. I always knew she liked me best.

Reasons

She spins out intestines into glistening patterns,
on the terracotta tiles of the pantry floor
while preparing chicken.
She sifts through them,
trying to account for last night's argument.

Weeks ago I found her scrying over the birdbath.
She said she'd seen my real face
while starlings picked at the white of her knuckles.

At the beach on Saturday I wanted to take her hand
but she collected sea shells; razors, piddocks, wide-mouthed whelks,
the pelican's foot, the auger shell.

She sprinkled them across
the opening to the Cave of the Deadman
and truncheoned them in with her fists.
I left her there, drawing diagrams, taking notes.

Jetko

She's doused for ley lines,
using an Egyptian ankh on a chain of fine filigree.
It seems there is a chasm,
a tear in space, a negative river of energy,
that hurtles along our croft and
through the house lengthways.
It cuts our bed in two.
Our favourite seats, my corner of the couch,
her winged chair,
are separated by it.
Our earthenware plates
divided by it.

Folks around here say you can tell your fortune
by hauling up a turnip under full moon light.
She's out there now,
naked, in a row of garden greens.

Jetko

Marise Morland-Chapman

was born in High Wycombe in 1947. Her father ran a dance orchestra and she herself studied ballet and the piano. She had an early interest in Science Fiction, writing it at school and later for the house magazine of her employer, Bucks County Library. She had various employment before supporting a full time writing career with temporary jobs, such as making circuit boards and as an artists' model. Her Science Fiction has received wide magazine publication, as has her poetry; she has won regional prizes and a Yeats Society commendation. In 1988-89 her comic strip *Time and Ms Jones*, in collaboration with artist Adolfo Buylla, was serialised by the Sunday Times and later received syndication in Europe. She is currently working on a novel *The Stars Entice*.

Screen Test

You and me, mum, at the cinema.
The film was "Picnic." I was eight.
Don't fidget, you said; but I loved it
(Almost as much as I loved you.)
Kim Novak was so pretty in her peach-pink dress,
Swaying on a swing, dancing to Moonglow,
Captivating the itinerant hero.
(She was almost as pretty as you, mum.
How I adored
Your long dark hair and green green eyes.)
Seeing the film again, just yesterday,
I remembered how I aspired
To being pretty. (To make you proud of me.)
Was I ever? Were you ever?
Never.
Time has shifted the focus. For me now,
The finest moment is the rebel daughter
Fleeing the grasp of her smother-mother
To pursue freedom and her drifter lover,
The Greyhound bus and the freight train
Thundering in parallel across the open plain.
Perhaps
If I'd been eighteen instead of eight
I would have seen my future there,
Beyond beauty's entrapments.

Morland-Chapman

Encounter at Park Street

Lost in the splendour of her eyes
He stands framed in stasis.
He cannot leave her,
Cannot cross the street.
Cars halt at the zebra, then move on.
Two Kwik-Fit men, blue-overalled,
Stroll by incuriously.
Youths carry beers from the corner shop.
A woman posts a letter.
The lovers breathe stillness, eyes locked.
His fingers cup her chin, smooth back her hair.
Her face, intense and studious,
Blazes with a sudden knowing beauty.
He is hers.

In her kitchen, my mother cooks dinner.
Ducks squabble on the river.
And trees on the horizon,
Changeless since my birth,
Continue their slow dreaming.
The world turns again. The moment passes,
Becomes one with the deep-rooted Earth.

Morland-Chapman

The Poet to his Muse

And you have gone your way
Heedlessly,
A butterfly in the mist,
Never realising
I gave you beauty.
I stood at a distance, watching
As you worked, head bent.
Each golden curl,
Each sweep of your eyelashes
Profiled in sunlight.
Innocent sorcery, free from blandishment,
Translated in my mind's eye
To ethereal grace.
Go, then; I can demand
No loyalty, merely re-create
Your image in my words.
Somewhere, others view
Your long-lashed eyes,
And kiss
Your apple cheeks.
I gave you beauty.
You seized my gift and fled.

Morland-Chapman

Reunion

She remembered (she told me)
Crossing the old railway bridge:
The steam from the passing engines
Drifting through the planks at her feet.
Each week we used to walk (I remembered)
Up through the cemetery to the playing fields;
Young, raucous, wielding our shoe bags,
Deriding the mute admonition of the headstones.
Once when I climbed the path
Workmen were pollarding trees.
Branches smouldered in little bonfires.
And now, from all the intensity of girlish trivia-
Crushes, agonies and fads-
Only the smoke endures,
Drifting,
As if in a dream of itself,
Above our departed school.

Morland-Chapman

Helen Buckingham

was born in London in 1960 and now lives in Bristol. She began writing in the early eighties and her poetry, articles and short stories have appeared in magazines and journals including, in the UK, *Mslexia*, *Staple* and *The Interpreter's House*; overseas her work has been published by *E2K* (USA), *The Mainichi Daily News* (Japan) and *Famous Reporter* (Aus). Her poetry has been performed in venues ranging from Jesters Comedy Club in Bristol, to the crypt of Coventry Cathedral and on BBC Radio.
Photograph by Richard Kevern.

Future Past

Silent night;
and he has gone to church
the usual way.

Whilst she
sits alone,
prodding at the video,
lodged behind the present pile
and last year's salvaged tree.

Tomorrow should be
much the same:
the neighbour's kids in polished mode;
the turkey hamper overload;
the Jimmy Stewart video.

Outside amongst the fairy lights,
another red-nosed Santa dies.

She offers up a mince pie
and a schooner of sherry,
before pulling the plug
on her new-fangled telly.

He'd sworn she'd get
the hang of it.

Little could they know.

It was Ruth Rendell's Birthday

Mine too.
The forecourt sky was gilt-edged blue,
the office bloomed Venetian blue,
the rings lay polished on their pyre,
a puff of powder blue;
we swore forever to be true,
for better or for blue…

But it was February.
And someone up there
knew.

Buckingham

Green Light

The girl from Bayeux with cars on her wall
is young, bilingual and knows how to drive,
I live with my husband - no car at all -
we meet in the hall, en route to our lives,
picking up pointers to disparate lands:
Monaco, Hockenheim......Bournemouth, Torbay;
I gather her partner lives near Le Mans
- she used to work at the Bayeux musee,
biding her time till her present career:
Trans-Euro Tourism - something like that -
gave her the green light to move over here,
net a new car and a short-tenure flat
- aeons away from that old tapestry!
I sigh as she taps the green light in me.

Previously Published in Konfluence #4 2001

Buckingham

the swans drift dream file
trailing lilies ashen light
into confetti…

                              sun beams
                              through the utility room
                              window….
                              she bundles in his dressing-gown

wedding ring
once removed…
a dead white rib

                              the lawn is tendrilled
                              vines entrap the twining trees
                              ivy binds the house….
                              stealing through the ruined fence
                              the *viper* renews her skin

Buckingham

Ocean View

beyond the pale egg wind-break rashers
strung out in the morning gloom
past the white loaf Pulling Palace

out the window me & you

Buckingham

Natasha Shakhnes

was born in Moscow in 1978. At the age of 14 years she moved to Israel with her parents and has lived there ever since. Her first successful poem was written in Russian but subsequently, with encouragement, she has concentrated on writing in English. She started writing permanently in 1998 with publication in magazines in Tel Aviv; she has also taken part in poetry readings organised by the English Department of the local University, as well as by the Israeli Association of English Writers.

an experience that was replaced

A man who knew several languages discerned a tone of sadness in one or two of them. He was moodier than ever aside a notion of defence that is applied without any efforts. There was a reason why it took him so long to correct his own errors but he had been skipping it forever without raising anyone's suspicion. He was unable to regret this choice if helplessness tore him apart only while it was described and he had never printed anything. For the men who didn't know how to fight their own scepticism any other obstacle would be a useless change. There is not even a single thread across their way of thinking until they find out that he calls everyone his saviour.

on a shaded foil

A master started passing further our once common cigarettes with a coat of words on them. A receiver in the middle had to translate the phrases one by one to let them turn into a fluent message. The speech seemed to be addressed to somebody I knew and sounded very bitter; I was unrolling filters without asking anyone to help me. What replaced them was a row of joints with dope and broken edges that as I felt the master would not let anybody finger. The speech was ending with some loops whose words were all the same; all the paths looked narrower than one used to find them but it was not because the leaves got bigger. I've got to remember that it's the last day I am here and no one should believe me if I say there is no way to know this.

Shaknes

a circular disorder

After a very late result of the last attempt one got to believe that he was unbreakable. Insights come to him when he is occupied with an exotic puzzle; they had never led to anything that he could not forgive himself. The local children were hardly ever shown the memorable places of their hometown and their open-mindedness derived from their parents' high awareness. People in the place where the puzzle was invented are exceptional because they don't find the insights too repetitive. One said it was his turn to take a holiday and surprised his colleagues that liked to be announced everything beforehand. Their customer was lonely because the people at the counter saw him making use of what had just been purchased.

Shaknes

a long apology

A few moments that a pair of essays had in common were so lucid that no space was left for any fun that people can't describe. Conclusions multiply if one says that he won't end up like a stranger's victim and he gave himself a promise that he wouldn't need this help next time. He wouldn't have to recognise his guilt the way he had imagined so far; it was a usual thing to point at some small but hopeless flaw on the face of a celebrity. Maybe no one but the star was to blame for this disturbing stature and the star reminds himself about that more than I have ever done it. A question if I can forgive him was a riddle of the deepest sympathy and to keep the world of my escape completely hazed for others seemed to be a wise protection. One gave up a leading role in choosing melodies outside the crucial scenes; all his thoughts stayed incomplete including a belief that such a state is threatening.

communication of saviours

A hall of viewers cried over a film not for its poignancy but because some other story should have been chosen for this morning. The one who didn't think how many times it had occurred to him discovers later on that if he hadn't spent them all with the only memory of his forgetfulness his life would have changed for worse. After compensating for a minor damage he interpreted the roommates' silence as forgiveness to hope that a misdeed behind his back would not be mentioned any more even if it leaves a trace somewhere. He learns to read the others' state and is drawn to their thoughts that concentrate on him; he knew it's what the opposition underwent as well.

As a conclusion each companion received an equal hand in a sophisticated cross; the names of two of us begin respectively with the first two letters of an alphabet. What made them even sound alike was a man whom they had been idealising and whose plans are known and explained. It's inconvenient to share them because the source of news is excessively reliable and the names of three of us start with the next three letters without replacing the first person's voice in our fellowship. A representative whose mind opposes any hierarchy shares nothing with a resident who grew up in a country that had based a law on this objection.

Shaknes

a dynamic temper

A passerby believed that many things could hypnotise him although he hadn't lived through them. Someone else could be acquainted to this person and still find his confidence surprising, he changed after an occasion when such a contradiction helped. He felt older in that respectful atmosphere among the minds that didn't know how he got there. He felt weaker and sat down to decide if his newest claims should derive from his experience. The armchair was soothing, it was clear that his package would reach its destination safely. For a while he didn't count anything and said 'Like an adult I knew how to send it'.

In a place where every cell can prove that no mistakes are made he started some arrangements just when anxiety was paralysing him. The exquisitely chosen time was praised with the same responsibility that let him remember the ideas. The one got a private phone and had to learn its signal; there could be a lonely older man who'd realised that the reaction depends on how much you practice it. He knew he wouldn't add a word for anyone even if he was near, he just memorised the signal earlier. Those who cannot work on their skills in any way believe that it's a reason why they hardly ever get a call.

Shaknes

Laura Sheridan

is compiling editor of *Pennine Ink Magazine* and is one of the founding members of its publisher Pennine Ink Writers' Workshop. The magazine has run since 1983 and has established an excellent reputation and an international readership. Laura teaches Psychology part-time and has a part-time job at a homework centre. Over the last eight years she has written twelve unpublished novels and about eighty short stories; her poetry has appeared in various small press magazines and she has won some prizes. Her reading covers exponents of fantasy such as Ursula Le Guin and Terry Pratchett, Science Fiction authors like Asimov and Stephen Barker, as well as Thomas Hardy and Wilbur Smith. She has been married for twenty-seven years and has two children in their twenties.

Eternal Opera

Sepia in redmist, he reaches the far side, racket
breaks in the backneath. He farsees under shaded hand - nothing
to be anxious about.
                "Got an aunt in Maine, she reads romances
and keeps tropical fish, but she aint got a fingerlength
of what's going on here; we're doing this to save her
from having to rake a life out of coffee grinds and peanuts, not
like these poor bastards who aint got two shells to rub together and
here we are, bombing the guts out of them - Agent Orange with a view -
and we're rubbing our arses on mangled roots, slitting skin
and strangling roosters with a blood red hand."
                                         His eyes are black
coal and the devil's shine; it's a fight to the last hangnail -
break and you're blasted - skinned to a corpse, but
you can't bow out, so play it, recite it, act it,
                keep singing the eternal opera.

Sheridan

David's Rooftop

when the song ended,
she was there, in his line of sight
and he was mesmerised by the floating veils
he watched
as she wove her way among the flowers
twisting and turning to avoid the sharp stones
and the city was dusty, his mouth
dry, the air full of insects and the
valley below scented with cedars

Sheridan

NOTES ON THE FOREST

Sounds
the stream is like a bath emptying
someone drowning

the light aircraft hums in the distance
the howl of the wolf boy
lawnmowing on a cold day

Sights
a bolt of twisted cloth
thick velvet and moss
a gown wrapped around the legs

she died in the forest
and has become overgrown with lichen while she reached out
for help

that tree has a sore belly button

a beast
its feet crossed, its toes splayed into roots, the claws
hidden amongst the leaves

Sheridan

What does the tree know?
The smell of the sky

On the ground
one angular stone
the stone is grey the leaves
are mustard, ochre, copper, chocolate, rust
the crinkled hair of the tree
or its flakes of dead skin

What might happen in the heart of the wood?
a body lies, half-covered in leaves
elves lurk with their feet on backward

Myth
if you place your ear to a knothole, you can hear the tree whispering

Sheridan

Being led blindly
the log on the ground was a dead crocodile
slimy and cold, fossilised
the branches of the sapling were the feathers
an emu's tail smelling of soil
and herbs

I took her to the hanging tree where the broken rope dangled but she said
it was only a child's swing
and the pine needles on the branch felt like plastic coated wires

she gave me a bronze age leaf

Smells
incense-the druid church
pine and smoky earth barbecue
dogshit

A question about a tree
Why do you live so rigidly?

Sheridan

The Rejuvenation Of Grandma

In the year 2153, Grandmas
were finally abolished. Peat watched
as the *Figmatron* agent
stuck his cigarillo in Grandma's ear
and all her cells began to regenerate.

But as her face plumped up
and her hair, fine and transparent
as optic fibre, began to turn cinnamon,
her clothes tightened and she gasped for air.

"Oh, Fylde coast," the *Figmatron* agent spluttered.
(By 2153 Blackpool and Morecambe
had become swear words
and Poulton was not to be mentioned in polite company.)
"We should have inverted her into lycra."

As Grandma began to turn blue,
Peat had a blinding flash of insight
"The vest," he cried.
"It's made of organic fibre."
MDF to be exact,
but finely woven for that smooth finish.

Sheridan

The agent immediately thrust his cigarillo
down Grandma's ever-burgeoning cleavage.
The vest, ingesting nicotinic acid and formic residue,
began to release its crushing grip and they
levered Grandma out of it.

"Thank Frank for that," she breathed,
covering herself with a few man-sized tissues.
"I thought I was going to die in there."
Who would have guessed
she'd turn out to be such a corker?
"See," she said. "Tobacco isn't all bad."

"The rejuvenating effects
weren't discovered until volunteer orang utans
were forced to smoke 1500 a day,
their toxin-filled bodies
crushed with formic residue and urea,
to form the basic elixir," the agent reminded her.
"Let us not forget their sacrifice."

The vest had now reached Peat
and was sitting up, begging for insects and arachnids,
although sometimes, MDF can be
partial to sponge cake.

Sheridan

Peat found a huge spider
under the tapestry of Leo Blair
being crowned king. He heard a crack as Grandma's teeth
exploded through her gums,
startling the agent
who, at that moment, had his tongue down her throat.

Yep, thought Peat - the future is neat.

Sheridan

Other Titles From Othername Press

Sleeping Rough In Dodge City
J C Hartley. **ISBN 0 9521806 1 8**

Mythic Cumbria. King Arthur at Maryport, Guenever at Carlisle, Grendal at the car-breakers and the Anti-Matter Man. Sex, stone circles and the Solway Firth.

It is terrific to read even a title like 'From Ratten Row Farm to the Black Lion, Durdar'!
Lord Bragg

Legislation Concerning Dreams
J C Hartley. **ISBN 09521806 0 X**

Leisure verse for the Light Age. Dream themed speculative and SF poetry.

I enjoyed this immensely and I recommend you get it.
The 'Exclusive'

"needs marinating"
Fanzine Fanatique

The Pennine Triangle Othername Press Poets: Volume One
Steve Sneyd, J C Hartley and J F Haines. **ISBN 09521806 2 6**

Alternative spin on M62/M60 Twilight Zone.

I heartily recommend this collection to all readers.
Anne Stephens. New Hope International Review On-Line.